First published in Great Britain in 2006

British Library Cataloguing-in-Publication Data
A CIP record for this title is available from the British Library

ISBN 1 84114 527 0
ISBN 978 1 84114 527 3

HALSGROVE
Halsgrove House
Lower Moor Way
Tiverton, Devon EX16 6SS
Tel: 01884 243242
Fax: 01884 243325
email: sales@halsgrove.com
website: www.halsgrove.com

Printed and bound by D'Auria Industrie Grafiche Spa, Italy

INTRODUCTION

The North Yorkshire Moors Railway is one of the earliest and most historic lines in the north of England. In order to improve inland trade links with the port of Whitby, and on the advice of George Stephenson, a railway using horses as motive power was built to link a harbour-side terminus with Pickering. The line followed a route to Grosmont, opened in June 1835, where it entered the valley of the River Esk via a 120 yard tunnel and climbed through Goathland to a summit of over 500 feet above sea level at the aptly named Fen Bog. From there it dropped into the stunning glacial gorge of Newton Dale descending this natural cutting all the way to Pickering. The whole route was opened in May 1836 and for almost a decade it operated in glorious isolation. In 1845 the York and North Midland Railway built a railway from York to Scarborough and included a link to Pickering. It also purchased the Whitby to Pickering line and rebuilt it, with some diversions, and to a specification capable of accommodating haulage by steam locomotion. Whitby was at last in direct contact with York, London and beyond. For over ninety years the railway transported people here and there on business or for leisure, and carried goods and chattels to meet the needs of the communities along the route. The arrival of the motor vehicle and an improved road system brought about reduced passenger numbers and the demise of goods traffic to such a point that the 1963 'Beeching Plan' recommended the closure of all routes to Whitby. Local protest managed to save the route to Middlesbrough but failed to halt closure of the historic route south and on 6 March 1965 the last trains ran from Whitby to Malton.

A small group of local people remained convinced that with volunteer help they could still operate the line from Grosmont to Pickering and cited the potential to attract tourists to one of the most historic railway lines running through a splendid National Park landscape. Purchase of the whole line to Pickering was beyond the means of the Preservation Society but then came support from the North Riding County Council which purchased the line from British Rail and allowed the Society to acquire it by payment in instalments over twenty years. This maintained the impetus that along with enthusiastic fundraising and much hard work resulted in the reopening of the railway in 1973 and regular steam hauled services again operating over the whole line in 1976.

The railway travels through a landscape of huge skies and dramatic moorland scenery where the weather can be exceptionally clement one moment and equally harsh the next. In winter a carpet of snow excites the photographer but emphasises a sense of remoteness that is easily felt on these moors. By way of contrast the line has provided locations for many films and television programmes. Goathland is the setting for Aidensfield in the hugely popular Yorkshire Television series *Heartbeat* and more recently was transformed into 'Hogsmeade' for the *Harry Potter* films.

Is it any wonder that the railway boasts being the country's most popular heritage line!

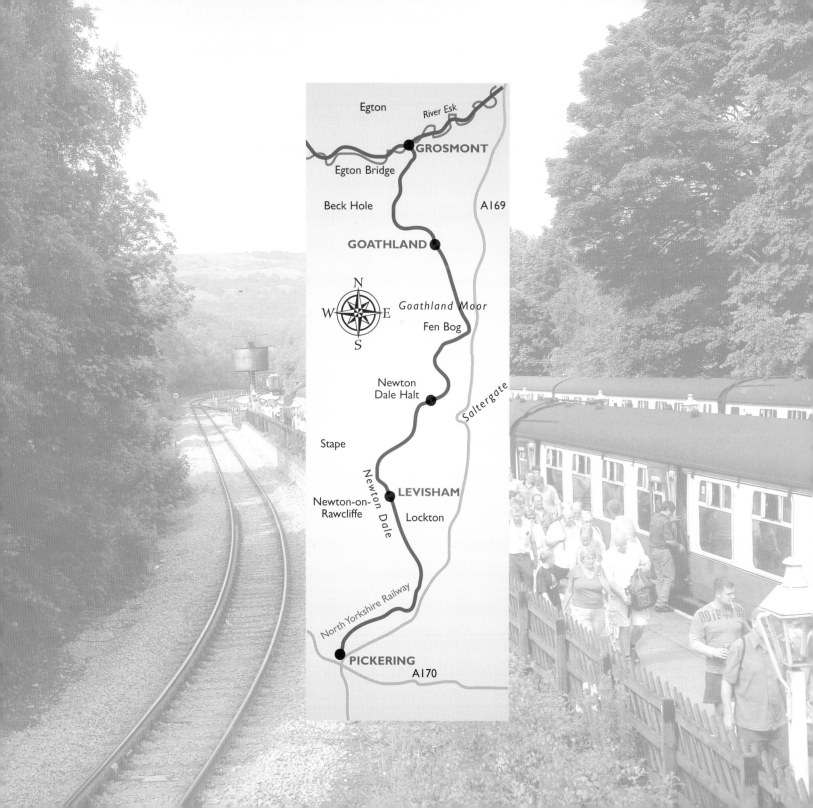

Grosmont is located just 6 miles west of Whitby. The village owes its very existence to the railway as during the construction of the tunnel through Lease Rigg, the hill from where this photograph was taken, rich deposits of iron were discovered leading to the development of ironstone mining and the growth of a little industrial community. The blast furnaces were in production between 1863 and 1891 but now very little remains, the site providing a car park hidden in the silver birch wood seen to the left of the footbridge.

For many years the station was extremely cramped and difficult to operate. In 1988 the Esk Valley line (Whitby to Middlesbrough), which uses platform 1, was re-aligned by British Railways allowing the Preservation Society to extend platform 2 northwards and this now deals with most arrivals and departures.

Platform 3 was converted into an island and on special event weekends demonstration freight trains can be viewed alongside prior to departure. The locomotive is one of two 0-6-2 tank locomotives on the line which were built for the Lambton Collieries. No 5 was built in 1909 by Robert Stephenson & Hawthorn of Darlington, retired from the NCB in 1969 and arrived on the NYMR the following year.

The superb signal box, opened in 1996, was constructed with bricks reclaimed from a similar structure at Whitby. An unusual feature is the two gate wheels that operate two pairs of gates, necessary as a result of the railway being twice as wide as the road. The gates nearest the station open across the road whilst those opposite swing away from the road to allow the train to pass.

All signalling on the line, which includes both semaphore and coloured light types, has been installed and is maintained by the Railway's Signal and Telegraph Department. Semaphore signals are either lower quadrant or upper quadrant and the NYMR has examples of each along the line. The lower quadrant signals date from the pre-1923 days of the North Eastern Railway and are identified by the arm being lowered from the horizontal 'on' position to 'off' informing the driver that the road ahead is clear. Examples of this type will be seen a little later at Goathland. At Grosmont upper quadrant signals are employed and as implied with this type the locomotive driver is waiting for the signal arm to be raised to the 'off' position to allow him to move away.

The driver of former London and North Eastern Railway K1 class 2-6-0 No. 2005 is checking that the crossing is clear as his charge backs into the station to couple to the coaches in platform 2. This locomotive includes amongst its claims to fame assisting K4 class locomotive No. 3442 *The Great Marquess* with the last train to run between Grosmont and Pickering on the 6 March 1965.

The upper quadrant is in the 'off' position indicating a clear road ahead for the lunchtime dining train special 'The Moorlander'. Diners on this particular service were lucky enough to be hauled by the streamlined ex London and North Eastern Railways class A4 No. 60007 named in honour of that railway's Chief Mechanical Engineer *Sir Nigel Gresley*.

On leaving the station the line almost immediately crosses a single span stone bridge over the River Esk, the parapets of which can be seen in the foreground.

Beyond the bridge the train will enter the 120-yard-long tunnel, built in 1865 for the steam railway to replace the original and much smaller one, built by Stephenson in 1836, for the original horse drawn carriageway.

(Photo. Karl Heath)

The route of the original line has become a footpath that leads through the now illuminated tunnel to the NYMR's Locomotive Department.

Opposite: The day of the October Gala in 1991 was greeted with superb weather conditions, particularly first thing in the morning. On that day I arrived early and was able to capture the locomotives being prepared for their day's toil.

Impatiently waiting for the off was former British Railways Standard Class 4MT (Mixed Traffic) 2-6-4T (Tank) No. 80135. This locomotive was built at Brighton in 1956, condemned to the 'famous' South Wales scrap yard at Barry in 1965, from where it was rescued and transferred to Pickering in 1973. (The scrap yard at Barry together with its owner Dai Woodham have cemented their place in preservation folklore. Their story has been told elsewhere; suffice to say that of around 380 standard gauge steam locomotives in the UK, 213 were rescued from Barry and of those over 120 have so far steamed back to life.)

For mutual benefit heritage railways often provide a base for smaller preservation groups and societies and the NYMR is no exception. One such organisation is the North Eastern Locomotive Preservation Group (NELPG) formed in 1966 with the aim of preserving at least one of the historic North Eastern Railway locomotives still operating at that time. They currently are responsible for five, one of which is LNER No. 2005.

With the last remnants of the locomotive's fire being deposited in the pit below, Southern Railway's 'Schools' Class No. 30926 *Repton* stands beneath the mechanical coal hopper. The railway can be justly proud of the fact that, commissioned in 1989, this was in fact the first purpose-built coaling plant constructed since the 1950s and thus the first in preservation.

Opposite: Readers of my previous 'Railway Moods' books will already be aware of my attraction to photographing steam after dark. Back in 1994 on the Saturday of that year's Gala I stayed into the night to take a few shots!

On that wonderful morning back in October 1991 the day's activities got under way with 80135 heading south to haul the first working from Pickering. The carriage and locomotive in tow would later be working the Pickering to Levisham vintage shuttle and are the subject of their own photograph later in the journey.

Opposite: Resting from their toils, many miles away from their former stomping ground, are former Southern Railway S15 Class No. 30841 and 'West Country' Class No. 34027 *Taw Valley*.

(Photo. Karl Heath)

A demonstration freight train climbs past the tiny hamlet of Esk Valley.

Opposite: The original horse railroad between Grosmont and Goathland included a rope-worked incline which saw use from 1836 until 1865. To enable steam traction to operate the line the incline had to be by-passed and a new route was built from just south of Grosmont Tunnel linking into the original route near Moorgates. The gradient of this deviation at 1 in 49 is still one of the steepest rail gradients in the country and locomotives have to work hard all the way to Goathland.

(Photo. Karl Heath)

The wonderfully varied scenery combined with the sight, to say nothing of the sound, of trains tackling the steep gradients attracts photographers from all over the country. The panoramic view over Esk Valley being one of several where those recording scenes on video are amply rewarded.

Opposite: The terrace of cottages at Esk Valley was built for workers at an ironstone mine that operated from 1860 to1876. There was no proper road access to the cottages until 1951 when the residents themselves funded the construction of a tarmac road. Prior to this the community had to rely on the branch line that ran along the original railway's track bed over which a fortnightly train travelled to deliver essential supplies.

(Photo. Karl Heath)

Stills photographers are attracted to the next section at Green End.

Opposite: This demonstration freight train is crossing the River Eller Beck at Water Ark. An interesting feature at this location, hidden by the foliage, is a footbridge that also straddles the river under the railway bridge.

For the short section between Beckhole and Darnholm the line swings to run west to east and actually crosses the river three times in quick succession. From the path that leads down to the footbridge is a splendid view of the trains as they continue their climb towards Goathland. Get the angle right and you can include the glow from the firebox in the picture.

Opposite: Viewed from the 'top' road down to Goathland, the steam locates the train deep in the cutting seen in the previous photograph. In the background is Egton High Moor.

This is another location favoured by photographers particularly for the early morning trains. Most position themselves, as I did, on the higher ground. However on this occasion one fellow snapper followed my own usual tendency to find a vantage point away from the crowd. Can you spot him in the bracken?

Opposite: At Darnholm the line returns to its southerly direction as the river is crossed for a fourth time in just half a mile.

Nowhere is the steepness of the unrelenting climb more discernable that on the final approach to the station at Goathland. Compare the slope of the track with the level coping stones topping the wall on the right. Disappearing over the hill on the right is the footpath that leads to the location from where the photographs at Darnholm were taken.

Viewed from the end of the platform, on a much brighter day, Southern Railway Class S15 No. 825 passes the point that marks the end of 3 miles of unbroken 1 in 49 gradient as it slows for the Goathland stop.

Goathland Station is the 'newest' station on the railway, built on the deviation line to serve the ever increasing needs of the developing local community. Its design is typical of the North Eastern Railway providing a home for the Station Master, a goods shed, coal and lime drops plus a weighbridge.

On a crisp winter's day in sub-zero temperatures the stark stonework contrasts sharply with the frost laden landscape.

(Photo. Karl Heath)

NOTICE. This BRIDGE is insufficient to carry a HEAVY MOTOR CAR The Registered Axle Weight of any axle of which exceeds THREE TONS or the Registered Axle-Weights of the several axles of which exceed in the aggregate FIVE TONS or a Heavy Motor Car drawing a TRAILER if the Registered Axle-Weights of the several Axles of the HEAVY MOTOR CAR and the Axle-weights of the several Axles of the TRAILER Exceed in the aggregate FIVE TONS

NORTH EASTERN RAILWAY COY YORK

MOTOR CAR ACTS 1896 AND 1903

The station has changed little since it was first opened on 1 July 1865 and is a delightful period piece with little trinkets of railway history scattered all around the site. For those unfamiliar with the Motor Car Acts of 1896 and 1903, there is a timely reminder by the bridge on the station approach road.

Opposite: Views of the station and the village have become familiar to millions of television viewers thanks to the hugely popular *Heartbeat* series in which Goathland takes on the guise of the fictional 'Aidensfield'. Maintaining links with the programme during the railway's 1960s Weekend, in 2005, vehicles from the show were displayed in front of the restored coal and lime drops.

The station has also appeared in a number of blockbuster movies. For the films based on J. K. Rowling's *Harry Potter* books it became 'Hogsmeade' where the school of wizardry and witch-craft is based. The shop (right) was transformed into the 'Prefect's Room' and the Ladies toilets have been used as the 'Wizard's Room' which I believe caused a certain amount of confusion at the time!

Up until the end of 2005 I had visited the area many times over the previous fifteen years but my portfolio of photographs lacked examples taken in the depth of winter. That was to change when heavy snowfall on 28 December was followed by a freezing cold but bright 29th. My younger son, Karl, and I braved the arctic temperatures and travelled across the Pennines to be rewarded with spectacular scenes such as this!

The same scene after 'global warming'!

Opposite: Moments later that day's 'Moorlander' dining train thundered into the station. What a memorable day for those lucky passengers enjoying a traditional Yorkshire dinner whilst travelling behind a steam locomotive across the snow carpeted moors at Christmas!

The role of the signalman is to ensure the safe running of the trains on the single track line by giving the driver the appropriate staff or token, the duty he is about to perform here.

He then returns to the signal box and checks with the next signalman that the line ahead is clear. A positive response and the signal (lower quadrant here) is dropped to give the 'right-away'.

North Eastern Railway J27 Class 0-6-0 locomotive No. 65894 was built in 1923 and worked in the North East of England until the end of steam in 1967. The NELPG's initial quest to preserve a working locomotive native to the area was successfully completed with the purchase of this J27 on 13 November 1967. In the siding stands a visitor from the Keighley and Worth Valley Railway, ex Lancashire and Yorkshire Saddletank No. 51218. These diminutive little engines were built to shunt the dock lines at Fleetwood, Liverpool and Goole.

(Photo. Karl Heath)

Pulling away from the station is another visitor from the Keighley and Worth Valley Railway, British Rail Standard Class 2MT No. 41241. This particular locomotive cemented its place in preservation history by hauling the inaugural train when the Worth Valley line re-opened back in June 1968.

With the line's summit still some distance away locomotives still have some work to do and heavy trains are at times double headed.

Opposite: Departures are therefore spirited to say the least but on that bitterly cold day in December the 'Moorlander' dining train put on a stunning show.

With a second locomotive providing banking assistance at the rear the display was a stirring sight.

This double-headed Pickering-bound train is just about to cross Eller Beck once more and pass the site of Abbot's House which marks the first recorded settlement of monks in Goathland in 1100.

The area around Goathland has been referred to as a green jewel in a sea of moorland, the reason for which is clear to see in this panoramic view from the A169 above the village. The train is approaching Moorgates.

Moorgates is another location popular with lineside photographers due in no small way to the ease of access by car. The road south from Goathland village towards Moorgates provides many vantage points from where afternoon trains can be photographed.

There is a public footpath running parallel to the railway here affording even more photographic opportunities. This particular shot was a challenge as I was not expecting a double header and only just managed to freeze the action of the pair between the trees in the foreground.

Opposite: Moorgates is the only place on the railway where a public road, that from Goathland, passes beneath the line.

For a perfect silhouette you need the sun to have descended to a level just above the track at the same time as the train is passing across the frame in the viewfinder. Believe me there are more failures than successes!

My favourite photograph from our Christmas 2005 visit and unfortunately, for me, it was taken by Karl! For much of the day sections of the railway were shrouded with mist with the sun continually battling to break through. Here the sun has lit the frost encrusted trees in the foreground whereas the mist has given the locomotive a ghost-like appearance as it drifts across the background. (I was located a little further up the line and saw, and photographed, nothing in the mist!)

58

At Moorgates the line leaves the oasis of green farmland behind as the landscape takes on the much more recognised moorland appearance.

Continuing the ascent towards the line's summit the train passes beneath an autumnal Goathland Moor in October 1991.

Locomotive No. 901 was for several years in the 1920s based at Hull Dairycoates to haul heavy coal trains to the docks from the South Yorkshire coalfield. During the Gala in October 1992 it was coupled to half a dozen 21-ton coal hopper wagons to recreate its former role.

Nowadays Fen Bog is a nature reserve which boasts a unique mixture of plants attracting dragonflies and many bird species to the area.

The North Yorkshire Moors National Park is reputed to have the largest tract of heather moorland in England and Wales. The carpet of colour that welcomes visitors in August reinforces this claim.

(Photo. Karl Heath)

Just to the east of Fen Bog is the locally named 'sand castle' which is actually the Early Warning Station of Fylingdales. Since becoming operational in 1964 this radar station has been gazing into space twenty-four hours a day (an activity quite common in the sixties!). The 'pyramid' that now stands on the skyline replaced the original spherical radomes that resembled giant golf balls and caused no end of debate as to their visual impact in a National Park.

The weather on the moors can be harsh at any time of year but especially in winter. What is photographically a wonderful sight must be a nightmare for those that have to earn their living from the land.

(Photo. Karl Heath)

Nestling below the cliffs of Huggitt's Scar, where the sides of Newton Dale become steep and dramatic, is Kidstye Farm where the train will slow and whistle its approach to the crossing.

Opposite: At long last the train we saw in the distance on page 61 has arrived at the summit. At the northern edge of the bog the line crosses the Lyke Wake Walk, the route of which is denoted by the intermittent line seen climbing the moor above the last four coaches. This is a long distance footpath across the moors from Osmotherly to Robin Hood's Bay.

For the geographers Newton Dale Gorge is 400 feet deep and was formed a mere 10,000 years ago, being a glacial over-flow channel. Melting ice which began as a trickle became a flow and finished as a raging torrent with millions of gallons of water carving its way through the then landscape creating this natural wonder. Three cheers for nature!

Overlooking the railway as it runs south from Newton Dale Halt is Skelton Tower. Looking every inch like the ruin of an ancient castle keep it was in fact built around 1850 by the Reverend Robert Skelton, the vicar of Levisham. It is claimed that he came here to write his sermons and occasionally quench his thirst!

The view of the tower when approaching via the moorland path from Levisham is as nothing to that from the tower itself which is spectacular…

Opposite: …whether seen on a mid-summer's day…

Opposite: ...or on a bitterly cold midwinter's afternoon.

The forest road from Levisham Station gives access to many walks and there are several that cross the railway requiring vigilance from both walkers and footplate crews. Whistling on the approach to one such crossing is former War Department 2-10-0 locomotive No. 3672 *Dame Vera Lynn*.

Passing the same location in more autumnal surroundings is LNER Class A2 4-6-2 No. 60532 *Blue Peter*. Built in 1948 for express work on East Coast Main Line it spent much of its working life in Scotland, eventually being withdrawn in 1966. Initial restoration work culminated with a renaming ceremony at Doncaster Works Open Day in 1971, the honour carried out by the then presenters of the BBC Blue Peter programme which I recall 'adopted' the locomotive for a few years. However the origin of the name was actually the winner of the 1939 Derby!

The home locomotive fleet is often bolstered by visitors to provide added interest especially on special event weekends. With steam to spare on the final approach to Levisham Station is ex Southern Region 'Battle of Britain' Class No. 34072 *257 Squadron* which spent the summer of 1991 in North Yorkshire.

The same location viewed from alongside the road crossing by the station.

Observed from the crossing itself, visiting LMS 4F 0-6-0 No. 4422 eases towards the platform with a fully loaded Gala day train. Note the trap points which are set to derail any train that might attempt to gain access to the single track north without the appropriate token for that section of line. This is a signalling safety device to prevent head on collisions on single track railways.

A closer look at the former War Department locomotive No. 3672. In 1944, following its construction in Glasgow, it was shipped to Egypt, along with 15 others to be placed in store. By October the following year they were all declared surplus to requirements and sold to the Hellenic State Railways of Greece where it worked until withdrawal in 1979. Repatriated by a number of enthusiasts it visited several preserved railways before settling on the NYMR in 1986. A full restoration was carried out and the locomotive entered service in 1989 amassing over 100,000 miles before being taken out of traffic for a rest and further overhaul in 1998.

The location of Levisham Station, some 1½ miles from the village it purported to serve, was dictated by the previously mentioned local land owner, and Lord of the Manor, the Reverend Robert Skelton (1792-1877). He had built a property nearby, Grove House, and wanted the station adjacent to it, so he provided the land.

The Levisham Station Group of volunteers have published *A Brief History* booklet which gives a fascinating insight into the care and attention to detail that preservationists give to their restoration projects. The main structures on the 'up' platform (towards London), the signal box, booking office and waiting shelter all date back to around 1880 and were left stripped and derelict when the line closed in 1965.

The Station House stands alongside, and at a slight angle to, the 'down' platform and has had starring roles in film and television. It was the 'Melton Carbury' of *Brideshead Revisited* and detectives Poirot and Sherlock Holmes have found vital clues in the area. My wife, Shirley, seen quietly reading, probably the latest Inspector Morse case, tells me that the station's Ladies waiting room is the first she has seen that has its own visitor's book. I don't recall one in the Gents!

For the 'Sixties Weekends' an open invitation is extended to individuals and organisations to display their own vintage transport exhibits. For the 2005 event an impressive line up of motor bikes was set against the goods dock siding.

Opposite, cars of all ages were parked up.

A double-headed departure viewed from alongside the station's Camping Coach (left) which was installed with all necessary services in 2004. Holidaymakers lucky enough to be staying here have a lovely view along the valley.

Opposite: At Levisham little has changed over the years and the same can be said of the design of the NER Class J72 locomotives represented here by No.69023. Although this particular example is a relative youngster having been built in 1951, the first of the class had rolled out of the works fifty-four years earlier. The vintage coach attached is a former NER Inspection Saloon which was visiting from the Keighley and Worth Valley Railway where in the late sixties it starred as the 'Old Gentleman's Coach' in the original *Railway Children* motion picture.

At Farwath there remain two early cottages, provided by the original railway company to house their track workers. Special market-day trains would stop here to take the women-folk and goods to Pickering market.

Opposite: The road away from the station climbs steeply as it meanders its way towards the village and the progress of Pickering-bound trains can be followed from a number of locations. The last light of a murky winter's day picks out the trailing exhaust from a mid-week Santa Special train as it pulls away from the station.

On a bright autumn morning a demonstration freight train has emerged from the National Park hauled by 'Black Five' No. 45428. This locomotive carries the name *Eric Treacy* as a tribute to the former Bishop of Wakefield who was an eminent railway supporter and photographer.

The popularity of the railway is clear to see as a crowded 'up' platform at Pickering greets the latest arrival from Grosmont.

Most trains use the 'up' platform which the Society has extended and partly raised. The North Eastern Railway footbridge is a preservation-period addition brought in from Tyneside and erected in 1996.

Pickering Station was built in 1845 and boasted an overall slate roof with a glazed clerestory until removed in 1952, although the Railway has long term plans to replace it. With the aid of Heritage Lottery Funding the station was extensively refurbished in 2000/2001 creating an extremely attractive well cared for appearance enhanced in the summer months by the addition of splendid hanging baskets.

On a dull mid-winter's day, with travellers remaining in the warmth of the coaches, a much more deserted atmosphere pervades.

Freshly fallen snow under a clear blue sky with full sunshine and Santa has delivered every item on a photographer's wish list!

A spur of the moment visit can often provide a pleasant surprise such as a visiting troup of Morris Dancers performing on the platform...

...or a group of individuals in period costume about to embark on a journey back in time.

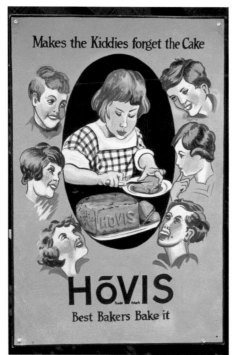

Once a year the railway as a whole takes on a 1943 guise as visitors are taken back to the war years to remember the railway men and women who gave their lives in the service of their country and the role played by the railways in defence of the Home Front.

The three-day event starts with the raising of the flag at Pickering Station.

All weekend re-enactment groups set up mock military operations up and down the line and the stations themselves capture the atmosphere of wartime with their blast-taped windows and sandbagged air-raid shelters. Local schoolchildren also get involved arriving at the station suitably attired with their gas masks round their necks and possessions in a suitcase, or pillowcase, in readiness for evacuation by train.

The scene may be from the forties but the 'run me over if you dare' stance is timeless!

The last of the day's sunshine highlights the tower of Pickering Castle which stands high on the hill overlooking the station.

Opposite: In December the station is in more festive mood to welcome children excited by the prospect of meeting Father Christmas on the Santa Special trains and Christmas lights and decorations adorn the buildings.

Dusk and the last train of the day eases away at the start of the return journey.

Approaching New Bridge on the morning of the October 2000 Gala is former Furness Railway locomotive No.20 which was originally built in 1863! It was visiting from the Lakeside and Haverthwaite Railway in Cumbria where its restoration had recently been completed.

On Gala weekends a vintage shuttle service often runs between Pickering and Levisham utilising the Railway's former Great Western Railway Inspection Saloon which was built in Swindon during railway nationalisation year, 1948.

Opposite: The return journey has re-entered Newton Dale Gorge as it heads towards Farwath. For the next 10 miles the route will closely follow Pickering Beck seen here meandering alongside the track. The forestation along this section dates from the 1920s when there was a national campaign to make Britain self-sufficient in timber production.

A train comprising a very mixed rake of coaches makes a leisurely, and environmentally friendly, departure from Levisham.

Opposite: In 1992 it was suitably paired with ex Great Western Railway Class 56XX 0-6-2 Tank No. 6619, another product of Swindon albeit twenty years earlier.

Opposite: However there are occasional exceptions to the rule!

Walkers having to cross the line have the benefit of an early warning system as the sound of the locomotives thundering up the climb away from the station can be heard resonating around the valley long before they come into view.

(Photo. Karl Heath)

113

Another view of No.6619 this time charging up the bank at the head of a north-bound train. These powerful locomotives were nicknamed 'Jumbos', because of their protruding smoke-boxes and like most of the class this particular example spent much of its working life on coal and local passenger traffic in the valleys of South Wales.

It is hard to believe but in 1929 Newton Dale was bare open sheep pasture. The first Forestry Commission foresters planted Norway Spruce and Douglas Fir, the latter of which have grown into huge trees. Over the years it became clear that the Norway Spruce did not grow as fast and when felled have been replaced with Douglas Fir or Sitka Spruce. All year round the forestation provides a wonderful backdrop.

With the ferns and trees that line the gorge in full bloom, the train scurries along towards Newton Dale Halt which lies beneath Huggitt's Scar, the flat-topped outcrop at the head of the valley in this view.

(Photo. Karl Heath)

116

The view from Huggitt's Scar on a glorious spring afternoon.

This photograph, of a northbound train pulling away from the halt, was taken in 1991 during one of my earliest visits to this line. Having parked alongside the A169 I totally misjudged the distance across the moors to this vantage point and well remember the feeling of complete isolation when having taken this one shot I turned and could see nothing but open moorland with no sign of life for what seemed like miles. It was a mistake that has not been repeated.

Taken from the A169, by Fylingdales, the disappointment of discovering mist in the valley at Fen Bog was swept away as it partially cleared to allow this ghostly scene to be recorded.

The more orthodox view from the same location.

George Stevenson, known colloquially as 'The Father of Railways' engineered the very first railway between Stockton and Darlington which opened in 1825. 150 years later during the celebrations to commemorate that memorable event LMS Class 5 4-6-0 No. 44767 was named in his honour.

On a crystal-clear autumnal afternoon the train cruises down the bank at Moorgates.

The last light of the day highlights the descending train in this panoramic view of Moorgates.
The Fylingdales 'sandcastle' stands proud on the skyline.

The lush green farmland that surrounds Goathland contrasts sharply with the harsher moorland on the horizon as the train whistles its imminent arrival at the station.

Opposite: Over the weekend of 18 and 19 June 2005 'Moors 65' celebrated the closure and rebirth of the line marking the fortieth anniversary of the year that the Beeching axe fell on the railway from Whitby. Visiting from the National Railway Museum was the very first Type 4 diesel locomotive constructed, D200, representing motive power in service around the time of closure.

Opposite: Passing the same signals on a cold December day was Black 5 No. 45212 which incidentally hauled the last scheduled British Railway's steam service in 1968.

With snow on the ground, frost clinging to the trees, mist swirling all round and the low sun perfectly positioned I couldn't resist taking this silhouette of the signal gantry.

127

Opposite: The signalman has just received the token from the crew of No. 45212 and will quickly return to the warmth of his box to await the arrival of the next train from Grosmont.

Whilst I was photographing the arrival from the road bridge at the southern end of the station Karl captured the scene from the platform. You will have noted that Karl has made a significant contribution to this album and it is only right that I should record my grateful thanks to him for his valued assistance, and advice, with the book.

129

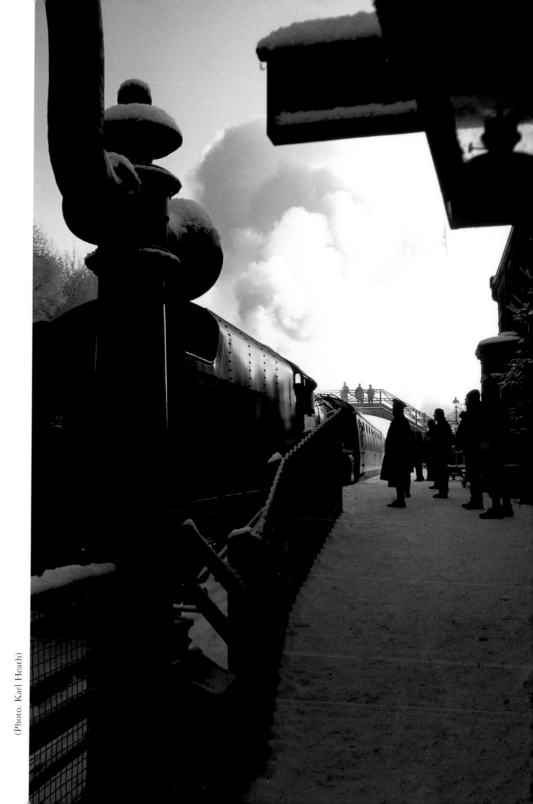

(Photo. Karl Heath)

A Grosmont-bound train stands in Goathland Station in much warmer conditions, and, to redress the balance Karl can be seen in this photograph. He is the tall young man with his camera strap across his white T-shirt standing on the platform on this side.

Opposite: As it happens, in this wintry portrait of the station again taken by Karl, minutes before the image on the previous page, the lonely shivering figure of your author can be seen on the bridge in the middle distance.

Fans of the television series *Heartbeat* make their way from the station to the village above, no doubt calling in at the popular 'Aidensfield Arms', which is the building seen at the top of the road.

An early morning freight train glides down past Darnholm heading back to Grosmont.

Believe it or not this freight train trundling along was photographed on the same day as the one opposite. The loss of sunlight changed the colour of the surrounding landscape dramatically.

Opposite: For the Autumn 2004 Gala the Severn Valley Railway's former Great Western 2-6-2 Tank No.5164 visited. The opportunity to pair this with the Railway's own Swindon-built locomotive was not missed and the combination is seen here passing through the cutting at Water Ark.

A freight working drifting through Green End is photographed from the original 1836 route which now provides one of the most popular walks in the National Park – the Historical Rail Trail.

Another view from the Rail Trail as a late afternoon passenger service passes the cottages at Esk Valley on the outskirts of Grosmont.

Alongside the railway's sheds and workshops the train is about to enter the tunnel on the final approach to Grosmont Station.

Oppoosite: The crossing is clear and the next train to arriving at platform 2 is the focus of photographer's attention.

(Photo. Karl Heath)

The journey is almost over as an early morning arrival coasts into the station…

Opposite: …and draws to halt alongside platform 2.

140

One such Summer Special heads back from Whitby.

Opposite: That completes the journey on the restored North Yorkshire Moors Railway. However for some time the Society has sought to reintroduce a regular service to Whitby along the adjacent Esk Valley line and in 2005 ran a series of steam-hauled Summer Specials on selected dates. So on certain occasions disembarking passengers will have the opportunity to 'change here for Whitby!'

There is much work to be done, and paid for, by both the Preservation Society and Strategic Rail Authority before trains can run directly from the Esk Valley line onto the North Yorkshire Moors line. However the prospect of a day trip by steam train visiting Pickering a busy market town, Goathland aka Aidensfield, and Whitby with its historic port and Abbey is an exciting prospect. I wish them every success and look forward to travelling on it and of course, the additional photographic opportunities it will provide.